FORBIDDEN FRUIT
CREATES MANY JAMS

Mary Katherine and David Compton

FORBIDDEN FRUIT
CREATES MANY JAMS

Roadside church signs across America

NEW AMERICAN LIBRARY

New American Library
Published by New American Library, a division of
Penguin Putnam Inc., 375 Hudson Street, New York, New York 10014, U.S.A.
Penguin Books Ltd, 27 Wrights Lane, London W8 5TZ, England
Penguin Books Australia Ltd, Ringwood, Victoria, Australia
Penguin Books Canada Ltd, 10 Alcorn Avenue, Toronto, Ontario, Canada M4V 3B2
Penguin Books (N.Z.) Ltd, 182–190 Wairau Road, Auckland 10, New Zealand

Penguin Books Ltd, Registered Offices: Harmondsworth, Middlesex, England

First published by New American Library, a division of Penguin Putnam Inc.

First Printing, August 2001
9   10   8

LIBRARY OF CONGRESS CATALOG CARD NUMBER: 2001018676

Set in Futura Book

Printed in the United States of America

For Sarah,
our own epiphany

Introduction

We fondly remember that Saturday afternoon in the fall, some-where along a two-lane country highway in North Carolina, when we experienced an epiphany: a white clapboard church, its doors locked tight, leaves swirling around the base of the sign out front as traffic sped by. We slowed the car to look. The church was obviously empty, yet this little church spoke to us, through the message on the sign: *Forbidden Fruit Creates Many Jams.*

We had a laugh and talked about other signs we had seen over the years. We kept a notebook in the car and began collecting these "sentence sermons" wherever we traveled. Thus, the idea was born for this little book.

In an overwhelmingly high-tech world, church sign maxims and admonitions such as these have remained a simple, effective way to communicate to passersby. Some may find the more forthright religious sayings humorous, while the contemplative may find deep philosophical meaning in sayings intended to be merely amusing.

The signs make you think. They make you smile. They beg to be told and retold.

We're still riding around, keeping an eye out for more additions to our list. Next time you approach a church sign, why don't you take a moment to look? Who knows—the blur in your rearview mirror might have been a message meant for you.

We hope you enjoy this soulful slice of roadside Americana.

A SUNRISE IS GOD'S WAY OF TELLING THE WORLD TO LIGHTEN UP.

Forgive your enemies—nothing
annoys them more.

♦

You aren't too bad to come in.
You aren't too good to stay out.

♦

Christians, like pianos, need frequent tuning.

There's no business like soul business.

◆

If you were on trial for being a Christian, would there be enough evidence to convict you?

◆

When you meet temptation, turn to the right.

God loves you, whether you like it or not.

✦

Come in and pray today. Beat the Christmas rush!

✦

Setbacks pave the way for comebacks.

Pray up in advance.

✦

To be almost saved is to be totally lost.

✦

Feed your faith and your doubts will
starve to death.

God answers knee-mail.

✦

Every saint has a past.
Every sinner has a future.

✦

Jesus is my rock and my name is on the roll.

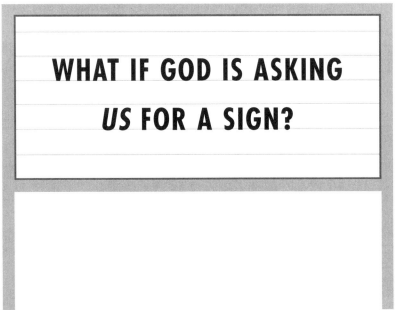

WHAT IF GOD IS ASKING *US* FOR A SIGN?

My boss is a Jewish carpenter.

♦

Want to avoid burning? Use Son block.

♦

We become like what we worship.

Don't give up—Moses was a basket case, too.

✦

If you want to cast a big shadow,
stand in God's light.

10

Words can't break bones,
but they can break hearts.

◆

By perseverance even the snail reached the ark.

A Bible falling apart belongs to
someone who isn't.

✦

Sin has no minimum wage.

✦

Man's disappointments are sometimes
God's appointments.

All's well that ends in heaven.

✦

God answers prayers—not advice.

Dusty Bibles lead to dirty lives.

✦

Jesus is my Prozac.

✦

Dark days are stepping-stones on
the path of light.

LORD, HELP ME BE
THE PERSON MY DOG
THINKS I AM.

See U in S NDAY SCHOOL.

✦

Don't be caught dead without Jesus.

✦

Creation bears God's autograph.

Count your blessings, not your problems.

◆

God promises no loaves for spiritual loafers.

◆

Home improvement:
Take your family to church.

Give Satan an inch and he'll be a ruler.

◆

We need to talk.
—God

◆

Big Brother: Jesus is watching you.

Under same management for 2000 years.

♦

Be ye fishers of men: You catch them,
He'll clean them.

Christians never meet for the last time.

✦

Average is as close to the bottom as to the top.

✦

Redemption: God's recycling plan.

FORBIDDEN FRUIT
CREATES MANY JAMS.

21

You can't slide uphill.

✦

Death is not a dead end
but a fork in the road.

✦

Life doesn't have any makeup tests.

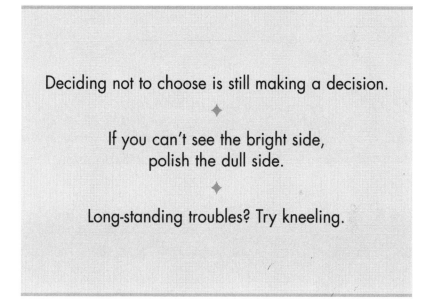

Deciding not to choose is still making a decision.

✦

If you can't see the bright side,
polish the dull side.

✦

Long-standing troubles? Try kneeling.

Many books inform.
Only the Bible can transform.

✦

Where death finds you, eternity will keep you.

✦

If you pause to think, you'll have cause to thank.

When you are the zero,
He is the one.

♦

Too many people saying "Our Father"
live as orphans.

♦

A backbone is better than a wishbone.

Walk with the Lord—you'll never be out of step.

✦

To hear God's voice, turn down the
world's volume.

✦

If you don't like the way the cookie crumbles,
try the Bread of Life.

God's lease on life never expires.

◆

Students: Come in and let us prepare
you for your finals.

◆

Experts made the *Titanic*.
Amateurs made the ark.

There is no right way to do a wrong thing.

✦

Salvation is free, but not until
you ask for it.

✦

You're on heaven's Most Wanted list.

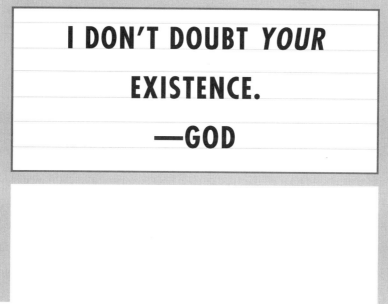

I DON'T DOUBT *YOUR* EXISTENCE.

—GOD

Spring—God's greeting card.

♦

Jesus—don't leave earth without him!

♦

Download your worries.
Get online with God!

Psalms read here.

✦

It's not what you know but
Who you know that counts.

✦

God grades on the cross, not the curve.

Jesus is an investment that never loses interest.

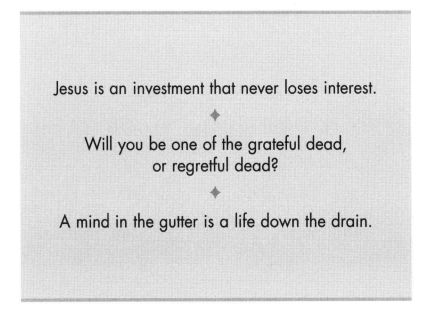

Will you be one of the grateful dead,
or regretful dead?

A mind in the gutter is a life down the drain.

When the devil reminds you of your past,
remind him of his future.

✦

A good place for the buck to stop is at the
collection plate.

✦

Born in a manger, now preparing us a mansion.

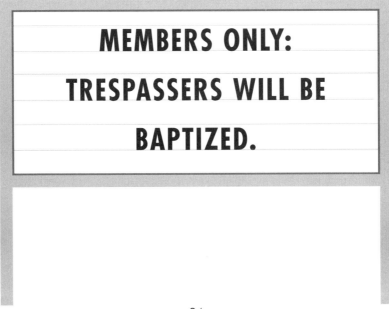

MEMBERS ONLY:
TRESPASSERS WILL BE
BAPTIZED.

Father knows best.

✦

The wages of sin have never been reduced.

✦

Peace is not the absence of conflict
but the ability to cope with it.

All our seats come with a first-class service.

♦

Dark clouds bring showers of blessings.

♦

Bask in the warmth of God's Son.

Can't sleep? Count your blessings, not sheep.

✦

A man who can kneel before God
can stand up to anything.

✦

We have a prophet-sharing plan.

You can't walk with God and hold hands
with Satan at the same time.

✦

Soular powered by the Son.

✦

In case of nuclear attack, the ban on praying
in school is lifted.

If you won't climb the mountain,
you can't see the view.

✦

Failure isn't falling down, it's staying down.

✦

Tense about the future? God is always present.

Grin! God loves you. Everyone else
will wonder what you've been up to.

✦

Playing with sin is toying with judgment.

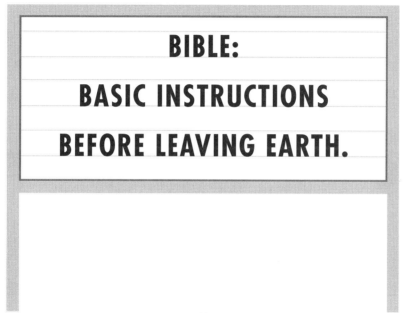

BIBLE:

BASIC INSTRUCTIONS

BEFORE LEAVING EARTH.

Backsliding begins where knee-bending ends.

◆

Christians aren't perfect—just forgiven.

◆

Don't make me come down there.
—God

Making a living is not the same as making a life.

✦

The Easter Bunny didn't rise from the dead.

✦

Hungry? Try feasting at the Lord's table.

Don't wait for six strong men to take you to church.

✦

A clean conscience makes a soft pillow.

✦

A temper displayed in public is indecent exposure.

We raise spiritual fruits, not religious nuts.

✦

Pick your friends—but not to pieces.

Heaven—don't miss it for the world.

◆

Can't stand the heat?
Better make plans to avoid it.

◆

Praying will give you a calm-plex.

This church prayer-conditioned.

✦

The Ten Commandments are not an option!

SOUL FOOD
SERVED HERE.

48

Jesus is the reason for the season.

✦

If you're headed in the wrong direction,
God allows U-turns.

✦

Weather forecast: The Son is always shining.

Give God what's right,
not what's left.

♦

Y1K caused the Dark Ages.

Read the Bible. It will scare the Hell out of you.

◆

In the dark? Follow the Son.

◆

Welcome to the perfect church—
for those who aren't.

Thank God for your dirty dishes.
At least you have food.

✦

Who lit the fuse for the Big Bang?

Running low on faith?
Stop in for a fill-up.

✦

Christ's return is near.
Don't miss it for the world.

✦

Don't crawl when your spirit wants to soar.

A CHURCH IS A GIFT
FROM GOD.
ASSEMBLY REQUIRED.

The prodigal son was having a bad heir day.

◆

Do you spell your best friend's name
D-O-G or G-O-D?

◆

Satan can't bring you down any farther than
your knees.

Life getting you down? Just look up.

✦

Do your best and Jesus will do the rest.

✦

Turn or burn.

What part of "Thou shalt not"
didn't you understand?
—God

◆

The worst prison is a closed heart.

Resist the Devil—submit to his enemy.

✦

When you're green with envy,
you're ripe for trouble.

✦

The tongue weighs practically nothing,
but few can hold it.

If you don't avoid the bait,
you'll end up on the hook.

◆

When someone gets you hot and bothered,
just turn on your prayer-conditioner.

Prepare and prevent rather than repair and repent.

✦

The best things in life aren't things.

Men: Hold your wife and kids
rather than the remote.

✦

Beware of the high cost of low living.

✦

Faith never stands around with its hands
in its pockets.

If you're ready to die, you're ready to live.

✦

Does your life shed light or cast shadows?

✦

Aspire to inspire before you expire.

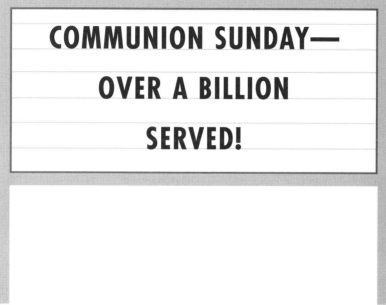

COMMUNION SUNDAY—
OVER A BILLION
SERVED!

The church: Band of the free, home of the saved.

✦

Rapture: One-way, all-expense-paid trip
for all eternity. No baggage allowed.

✦

People who fight fire with fire end up with ashes.

God so loved the world that He did not send a committee.

✦

Children need models, not critics.

TGIF—Thank God I'm Forgiven.

✦

God is everywhere so pray anywhere.

✦

Don't have anything to be thankful for?
Check your pulse.

Exposure to the Son will prevent burning.

✦

Seven days without prayer makes one weak.

✦

God gave everyone patience.
The wise use it.

When it comes to giving, some people
stop at nothing.

✦

God formed us, sin deformed us,
Christ transformed us.

✦

Peace begins not at a Mideast table
but at a Mideast stable.

KEEP USING MY NAME

IN VAIN, I'LL MAKE RUSH

HOUR LONGER. —GOD

Prayer should be our first resource,
not our last resort.

✦

A Bible in the hand is worth two on the shelf.

✦

Don't like how you were born?
Try being born again.

Does your spiritual house need a spring cleaning?

✦

I'm a fool for Christ. Whose fool are you?

Check up before you check out.

✦

Coincidence is when God chooses to
remain anonymous.

✦

Wal-Mart isn't the only saving place!

73

Ask about our pray-as-you-go plan.

✦

The Gospel is a declaration, not a debate.

✦

If you can't sleep, don't count sheep.
Talk to the Shepherd.

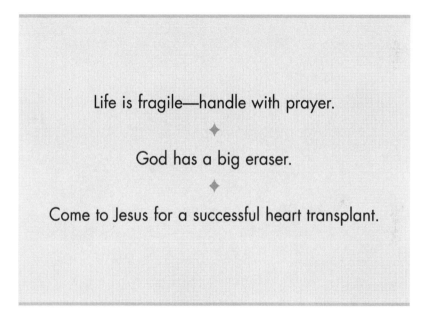

Life is fragile—handle with prayer.

♦

God has a big eraser.

♦

Come to Jesus for a successful heart transplant.

Have you read my #1 bestseller?
There will be a test.
—God

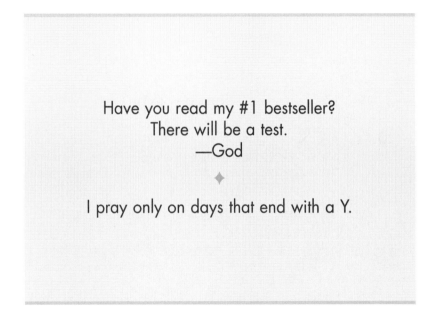

I pray only on days that end with a Y.

A lot of kneeling will keep you in good standing.

◆

A church alive is worth the drive.

◆

Take a God look at yourself.

In God we trust—right on the money.

◆

It's not the outlook—it's the uplook that counts.

◆

The cross is where love and sin meet.

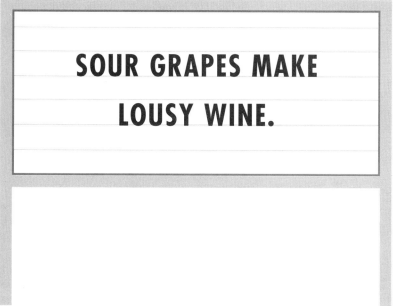

SOUR GRAPES MAKE
LOUSY WINE.

79

Tithe! Anyone can honk!

♦

The Bread of Life never gets stale.

♦

Many children are afraid of the dark.
Many adults are afraid of the light.

Jesus died on the cross—that you might get a life.

✦

We aren't Dairy Queen but our Sundays
are great!

✦

Praises go up—blessings come down.

On Judgment Day you'll meet Father God—
not Mother Earth!

✦

Don't like the Devil's fruit? Stay out of his orchard.

✦

We don't change the message. The message
changes us.

Money is a great servant but a terrible master.

◆

Friends don't let friends go to Hell.

It's easier to debate the Bible than obey it.

✦

In case of rapture, church will be empty.

✦

An upright man is never a downright failure.

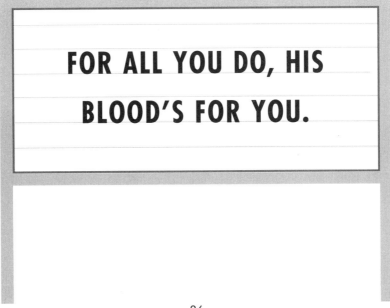

FOR ALL YOU DO, HIS
BLOOD'S FOR YOU.

86

Road rage? How would Jesus drive?

✦

If you stand for nothing, you'll fall for anything.

✦

Life is a measure to be filled,
not a cup to be drained.

Firefighters rescue. Only Jesus saves.

✦

God doesn't need great men.
Great men need God.

Be nice to your kids.
They'll be choosing your nursing home.

✦

All Christians work for the same employer.

✦

To avoid Sin's tragedy, learn Satan's strategy.

Plenty of people give the Lord credit.
Few give Him cash.

♦

Salvation: Don't leave home without it.

The Ten Commandments are not multiple-choice.

✦

Prayer doesn't need proof—it needs practice.

✦

Worry looks around. Faith looks up.

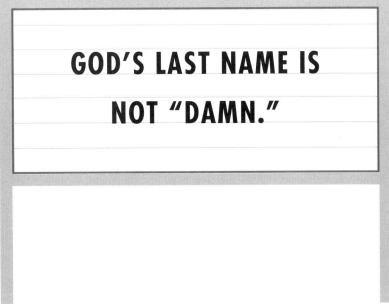

GOD'S LAST NAME IS
NOT "DAMN."

92

The wages of sin are death.
Quit before payday!

✦

To be lifted up, go down on your knees.

✦

God likes people—He sent his Son to be one!

The herein determines the hereafter.

✦

Get down on your knees and fight like a man!

✦

Nothing ruins the truth like stretching it.

Eternity is a long time to think about
what you should have done.

✦

We stand tallest when we stoop to help others.

No time to pray makes you easy prey.

◆

It's not just to wear the cross but to bear the cross.

◆

Little sins add up to big trouble.

We're too blessed to be depressed.

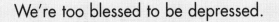

Jesus can turn your E-F-I-L around.

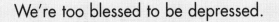

Big Bang Theory? You've got to be kidding.
—God

People we like the least need our love the most.

◆

God said it, I believe it, that settles it.

◆

Keep looking up. God is looking down.

Sore and weak from backsliding?
Try pew sitting and knee bends.

✦

Never give the Devil a ride.
He'll want to do the driving!

✦

God is always online. Never a busy signal!

The best Christmas gift ever was wrapped in a manger.

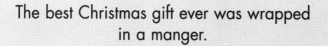

What did Noah do with the woodpeckers?

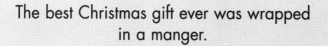

Be an organ donor—give your heart to Jesus!

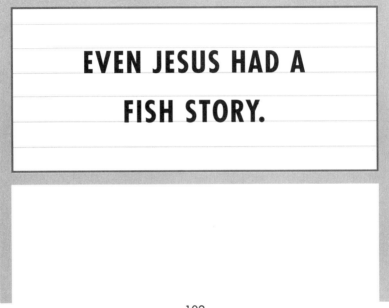

EVEN JESUS HAD A
FISH STORY.

God promised a safe landing, not smooth sailing.

✦

If at first you don't succeed,
read the instructions (Bible).

✦

Jesus built a bridge with two boards
and three nails.

103

Worry is the darkroom in which negatives
are developed.

✦

God doesn't want a share of your life,
He wants controlling interest!

The surest steps to happiness are
the steps to church.

✦

Children brought up in the church
are seldom brought up in court.

✦

A world of love makes a world of difference.

Happiness without reason is the ultimate freedom.

✦

If God is your copilot, switch seats!

Guests welcome. Members expected.

◆

The family that prays together stays together.

◆

April First: National Atheists Day.

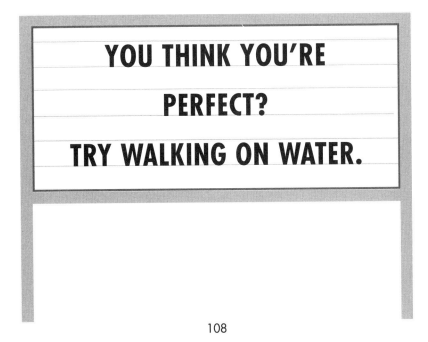

YOU THINK YOU'RE
PERFECT?
TRY WALKING ON WATER.

108

Thanksgiving is good, but thanks-living is better.

✦

Unplugged? Plug in and get current with God.

Going to church doesn't make you a Christian
any more than going to McDonald's
makes you a hamburger.

✦

Good old knee-ology is better than some theology.

Having a sharp tongue may cut your throat.

◆

At the end of your rope? Ask God to tie a knot.

◆

Kind words make good echoes.

Do you have any idea where you're going?
—God

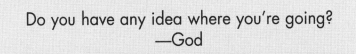

God made round faces. Man makes them long.

When the trumpet sounds, I'm outta here!

112

God's promises have no expiration dates.

✦

To know the strength of the anchor,
you need to feel the storm.

As long as there are tests, there will be
prayer in public schools.

◆

A man is tallest when he is on his knees.

◆

Redemption center—no coupons required.

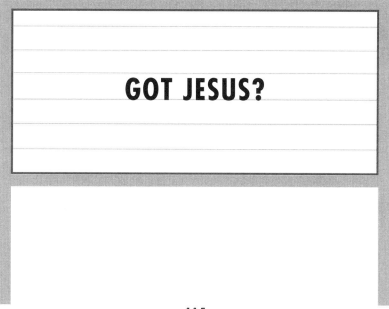

Sign broken, message inside.

◆

The greatest sin is not to take it seriously.

Try Jesus. If you don't like him,
the Devil will always take you back.

✦

Jesus paid a bill he didn't owe.

✦

The Light of the World knows no power failure.

Pride puffs you up. Love lifts you up.

◆

Rapture—the only way to fly!

◆

Don't look at the world through
woe-colored glasses.

118

Faults are thick where love is thin.

◆

CH??CH—What's missing?

The cross is God's way of making a
plus sign out of a minus.

✦

Rapture—separation of church and state!

✦

Don't put a question mark where
God put a period.

God is like a Hallmark card:
He cared enough to send the very best.

✦

Heaven is no trick and Hell is no treat.

✦

Strength in prayer is better than length in prayer.

God uses our down times to build us up.

◆

Grace happens.

◆

Decisions can take you out of God's will
but not out of His reach.

Lost? Come in for directions.

✦

The best way to have the last word is to apologize.

God has not gone on vacation and
left you in charge.

✦

It's hard to stumble when you're on your knees.

✦

Forbidden fruit may taste sweeter, but spoils faster.

FREE TRIP TO HEAVEN—
DETAILS INSIDE!

126

If there is no way out, there is a way up.

✦

The best antique is an old friend.

✦

One man and God make a majority.

Will the last person to leave please see that
the perpetual light is extinguished.

✦

If God seems far away, who moved?

His pain is your gain!

♦

Character is doing what's right when
no one's looking.

♦

Get right or get left.

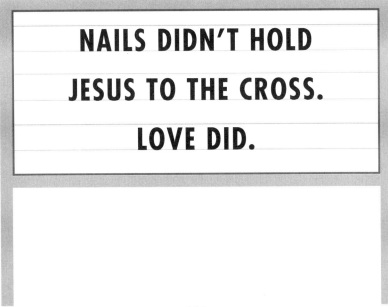

NAILS DIDN'T HOLD
JESUS TO THE CROSS.
LOVE DID.

130

If you're too busy to pray, you're too busy.

✦

Enjoy the day! Compliments of God.

✦

Prevent truth decay—brush up on the Bible.

Life is short. Pray hard.

✦

The church is a hospital for sinners, not a rest home for saints.

✦

Heaven: No pain, all gain.

When you fear God,
you have nothing else to fear.

✦

Exercise daily—walk with the Lord!

✦

Where will you be spending eternity:
Smoking or Nonsmoking?

I LOVE YOU, I LOVE YOU, I LOVE YOU.

—GOD

Mary Katherine Compton, a native of North Carolina, earned her Ph.D. at the University of Mississippi. She is an editor, and she is completing a book on the short stories of Eudora Welty and Anton Chekhov.

David Compton, born in Atlanta, was a marketing executive with several Fortune 500 companies before turning to writing. He is the national best-selling author of the thrillers *Executive Sanction* and *Impaired Judgment,* and is currently at work on his next novel.

Learn more about David Compton's books at:

www.davidcompton.com